# The Alphabet

In this section of your Buddy Book, you can write and draw pictures for each letter. You can also have fun reading the alphabet poem—from "Alligator sits, Butterfly flits" all the way to "Yarn soft and blue, Zipper–dee–do!"

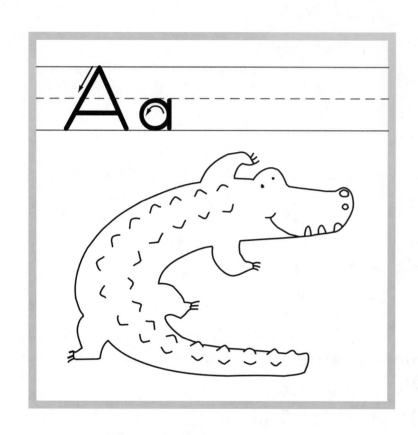

② Alligator sits,

Your Spot

**B b**

④ Butterfly flits.

Your Spot

Cup of tea,

Your Spot

Dd

Duck at sea.

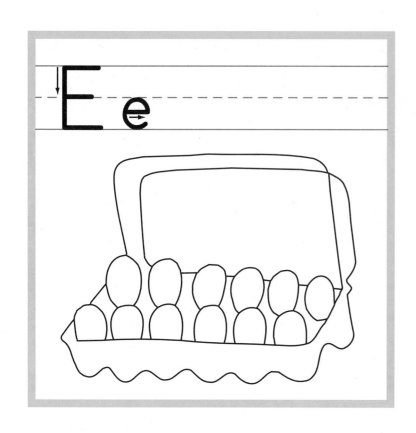

E e

Eggs to cook,

Your Spot

F f

Fish in a brook.

Your Spot

Girl named Mary,

Your Spot

Hat for Harry.

Your Spot

I i

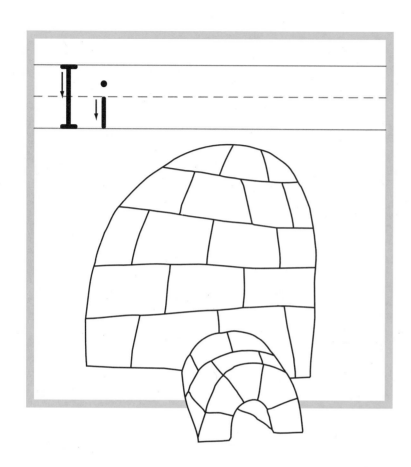

Igloo white,

Your Spot

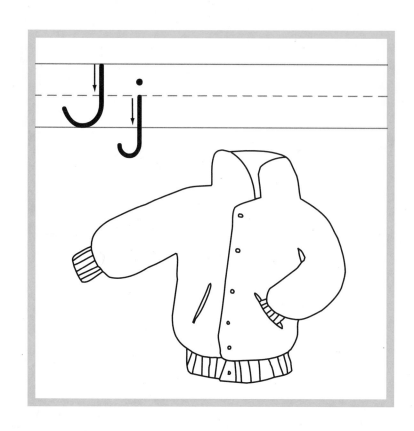

Jacket bright.

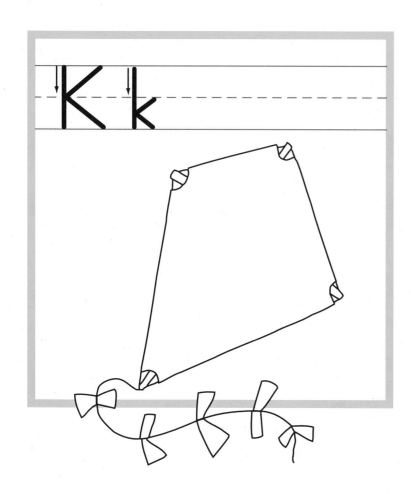

K k

Kite in the sky,

Your Spot

L l

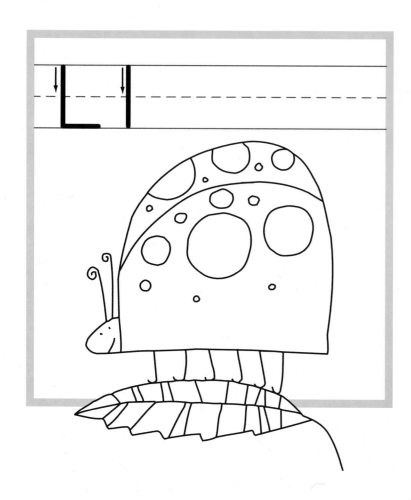

(24) Ladybug shy.

Your Spot

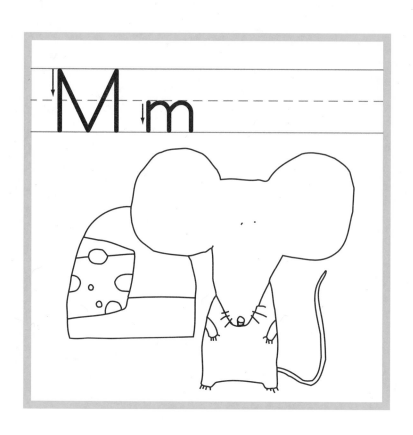

Mouse near a hole,

Your Spot

27

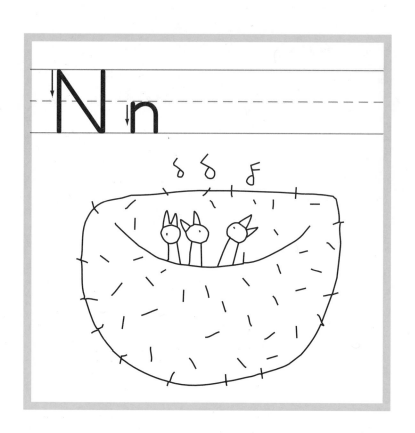

Nest like a bowl.

Your Spot

Octopus below,

Penguin in the snow.

Qq

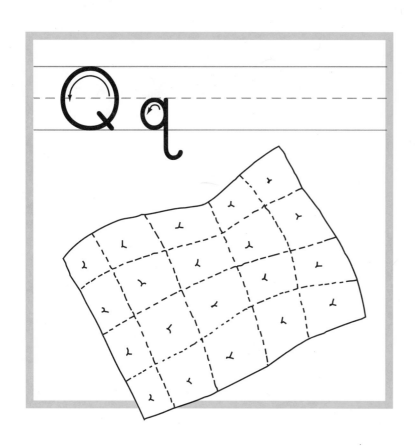

Quilt for a bed,

Your Spot

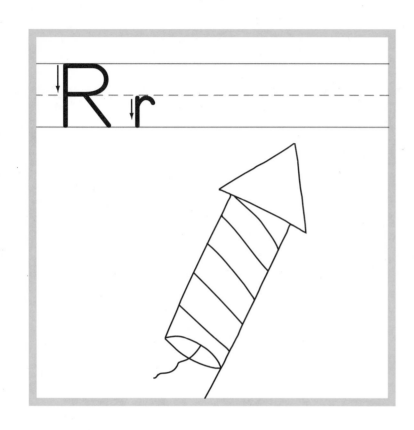

Rocket that's red.

Your Spot

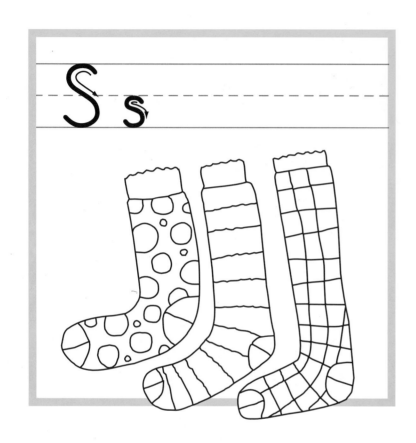

Ss

Socks for running,

Your Spot

Turtle goes sunning.

Your Spot

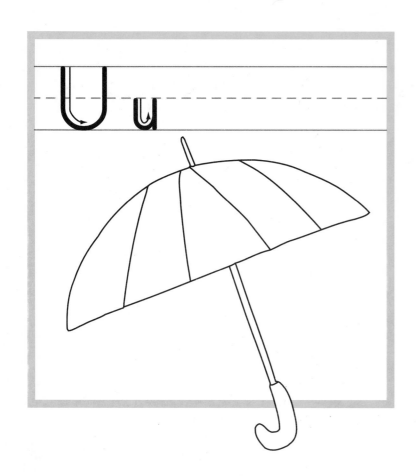

Umbrella for showers,

Your Spot

Vase full of flowers.

Your Spot

Wagon to pull,

Your Spot

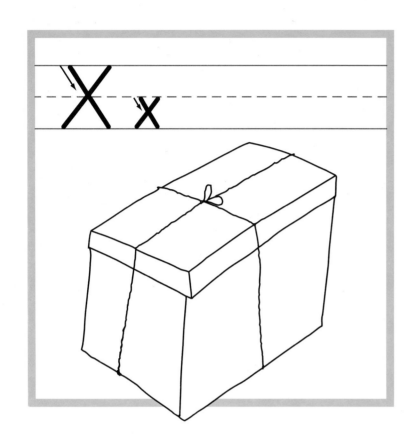

Bo<u>x</u> full of wool.

Your Spot

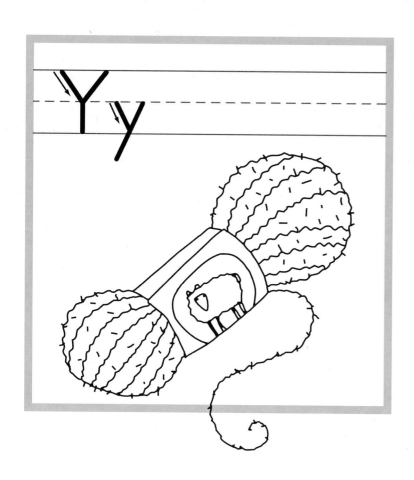

Yarn soft and blue,

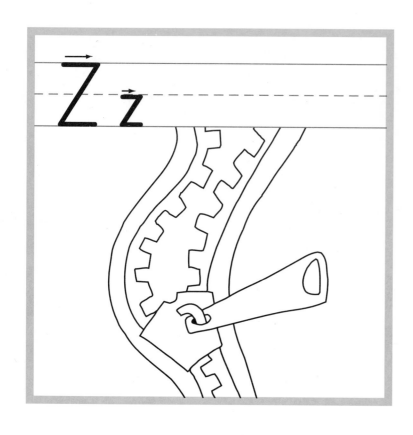

Zipper-dee-do!

Your Spot

# Alligator to Zipper-Dee-Do!

**Teacher:** Have fun reading these alphabet couplets with your young learners.

 Alligator sits,
Butterfly flits.

 Cup of tea,
Duck at sea.

 Eggs to cook,
Fish in a brook.

 Girl named Mary,
Hat for Harry.

 Igloo white,
Jacket bright.

 Kite in the sky,
Ladybug shy.

 Mouse near a hole,
Nest like a bowl.

 Octopus below,
Penguin in the snow.

 Quilt for a bed,
Rocket that's red.

 Socks for running,
Turtle goes sunning.

 Umbrella for showers,
Vase full of flowers.

 Wagon to pull,
Box full of wool.

 Yarn soft and blue,
Zipper-dee-do!

# Writer's Response

There are two kinds of pages in this section. The Writer's Response pages ask you to write and draw about the pages in *The Writing Spot* big book. "Your Spot" is a special place for your own ideas and pictures.

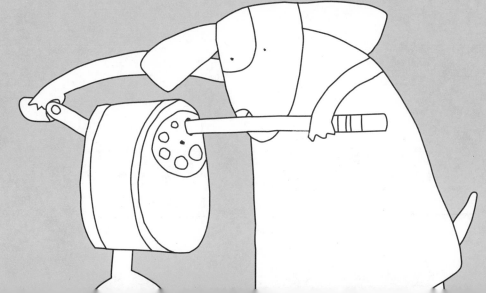

Writer's Response: Draw and name the butterfly that will hatch in your jar.

## Writers look and think.

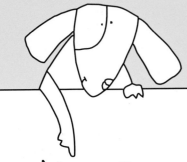

Your Spot

Writer's Response: Write something Spot might hear in your classroom.

**Writers talk and listen.**

Your Spot

Writer's Response: Use pictures and words to show one of your favorite books.

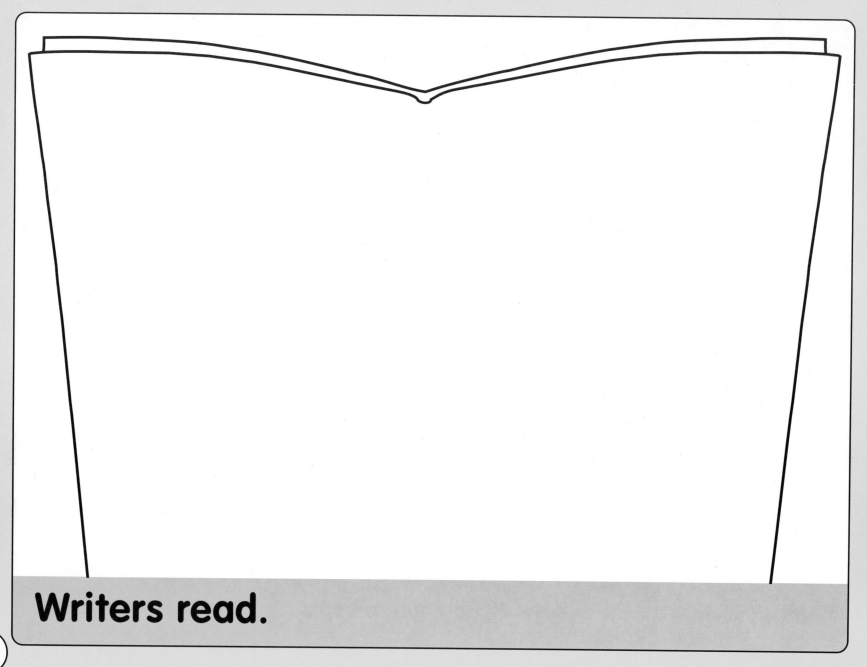

**Writers read.**

Your Spot

Writer's Response: Do your own writing here.

**Writers write.**

Your Spot

Writer's Response: Add words and pictures to show who you like to share your writing with.

**Writers share.**

Your Spot

**We send notes and cards.**

Your Spot

Writer's Response: Write a list for the crow, and then make a list of your own.

**We make lists.**

Your Spot

Writer's Response: Make your own journal page.

# We write in journals.

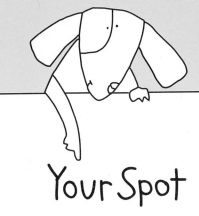

Your Spot

Writer's Response: Color these puppets and add one more. Then tell a story about them.

**We tell and write stories.**

Your Spot

Shhh

Thank you.

**We make signs.**

Your Spot

Writer's Response: Decorate this birthday banner with words and pictures.

**Happy Birthday to you!**

Your Spot

**Writer's Response:** Draw yourself and write a word that describes how you feel.

I feel . . .

Your Spot

Writer's Response: Add your friends to the clubhouse and write their names.

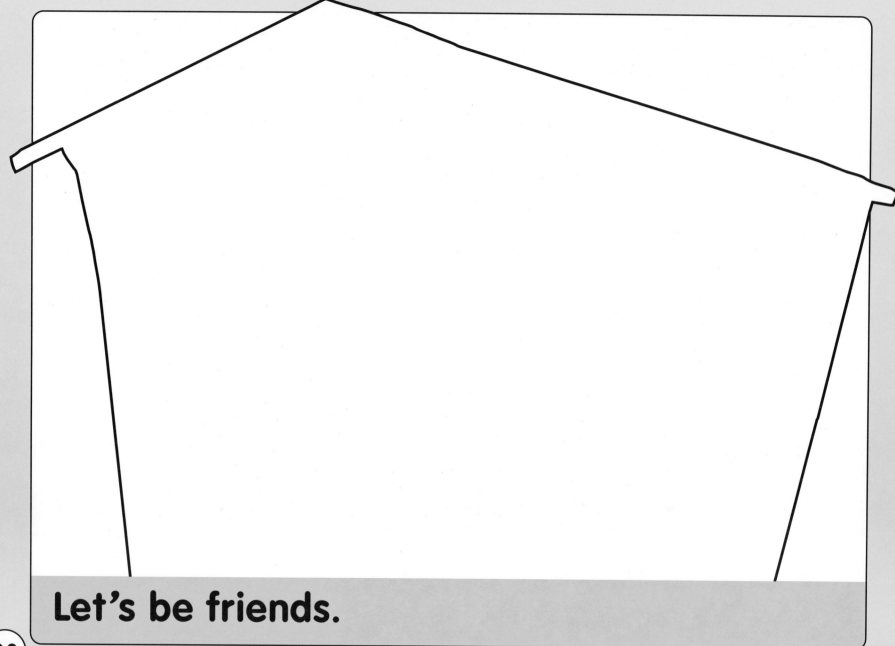

**Let's be friends.**

Your Spot

Writer's Response: Draw and label a healthful meal you'd like to eat.

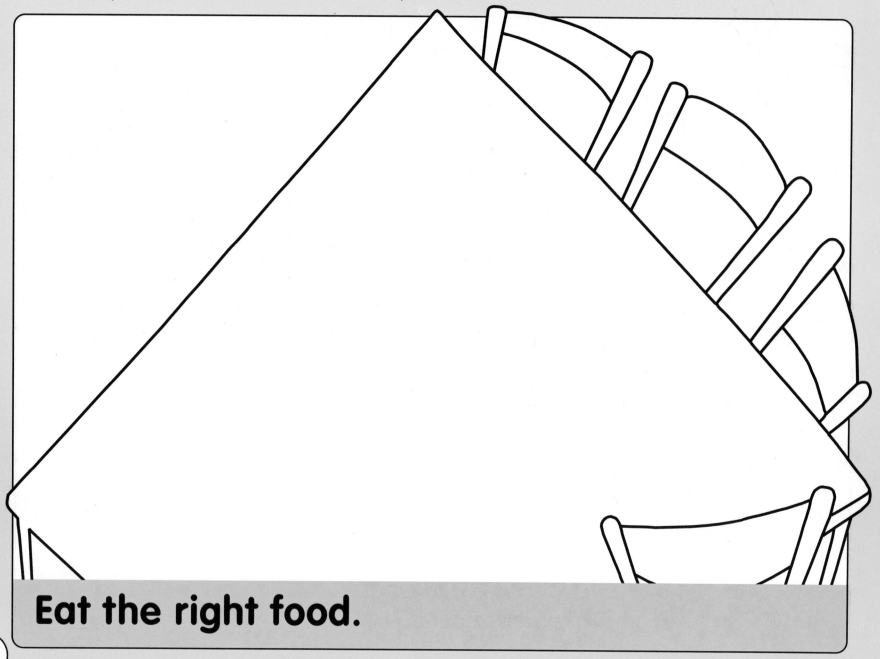

**Eat the right food.**

Your Spot

**Water is everywhere.**

Your Spot

Writer's Response: Put yourself in the space suit. Then draw and name a new planet.

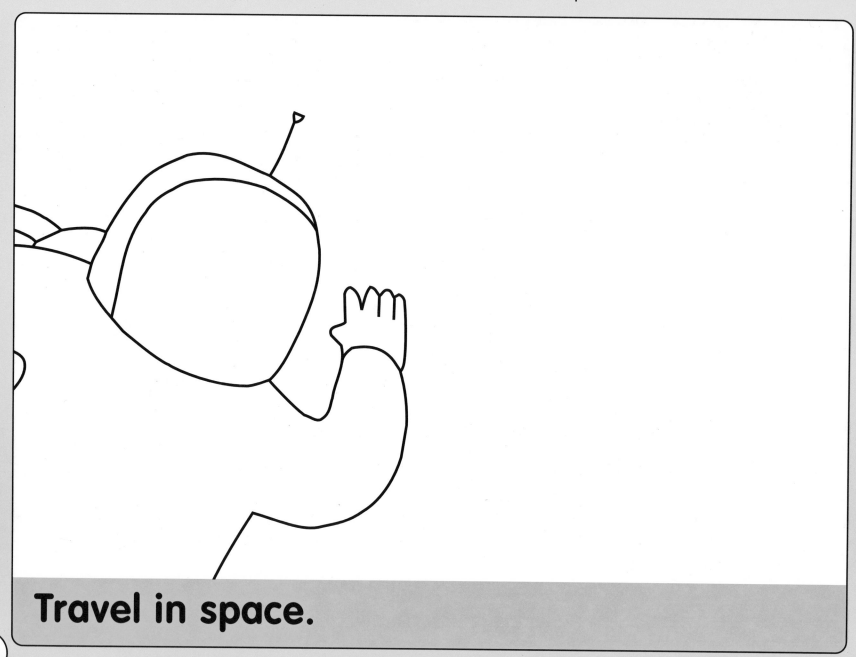

**Travel in space.**

Your Spot

**Writer's Response:** Draw yourself in the helicopter. Add a picture about weather and label it.

# What's the weather?

Your Spot

Writer's Response: Draw and label a picture about a color.

# Name the colors.

Your Spot

Writer's Response: Put yourself in the picture. Draw a favorite rhyme or write lists of rhyming words.

## Listen to the rhyme.

Your Spot

Writer's Response: Draw and write the name of a fairy-tale storyland you'd like to visit.

**Once upon a time . . .**

Your Spot

We hope you had fun writing in your Buddy Book. Keep writing!

–Your Book Buddies